"Lil, do you want to bike up a hill?" asked Dad.
"I want to sit still."

"Do you want to hike in the sun?" asked Dad. "That is not fun."

Lil Can't Miss

A Division of LeapFrog

Written by Suzanne Barchers
Illustrated by TRP Toons, Joe Yakovetic,
and Dave Walston

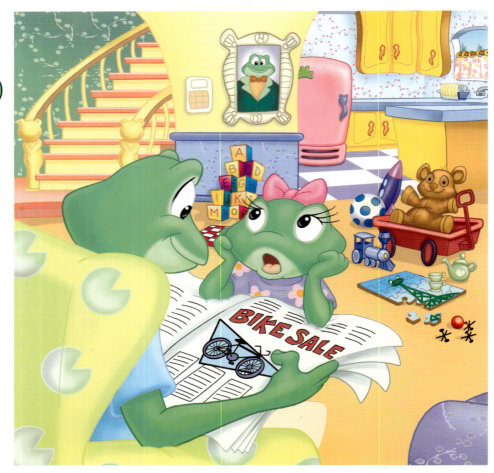

"Can you help me, Dad?" said Lil. "I am so sad. What can I do? What will be new?"

"Do you want to make a fine cake?"
"I don't want to bake," said Lil.

"Do you want to get an ice cream cone?" asked Dad.
"Not if I have to eat alone."

"Do you want to make a new game?" asked Dad. "They're all the same."

"Do you want to swim in a lake?" "I may see a snake!" said Lil.

"Do you want to dig a hole in the dirt?" asked Dad.
"My hand will get hurt."

"Do you want a new joke to tell?"
"No, I do not tell them well," said Lil.

"Do you want to ride in a truck?" asked Dad.
"I will get stuck in the muck."

"Do you want to pick a red rose?" asked Dad.
"It will tickle my nose," said Lil.

"Do you want to walk down the lane?" asked Dad. "I'd rather fly in a plane," said Lil.

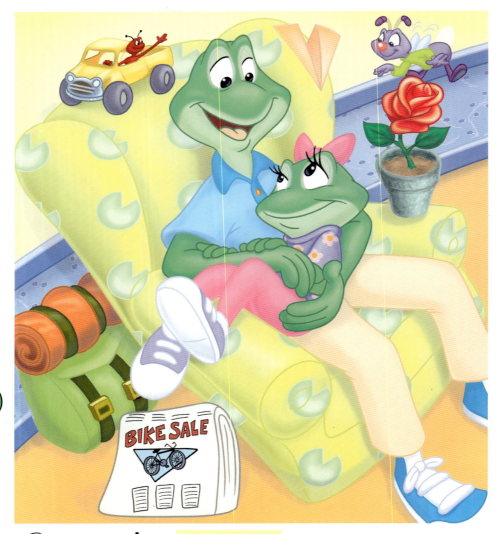

"Lil, come sit in my lap. I know you will feel better after a nap," said Dad.

Lil took a nap. She woke up with a snap.

Lil has new hope.
She will not mope!

Lil will ride in a truck and dig in the muck.

She will swim in a lake and bake a big cake.

She will pick a red rose to sniff with her nose.

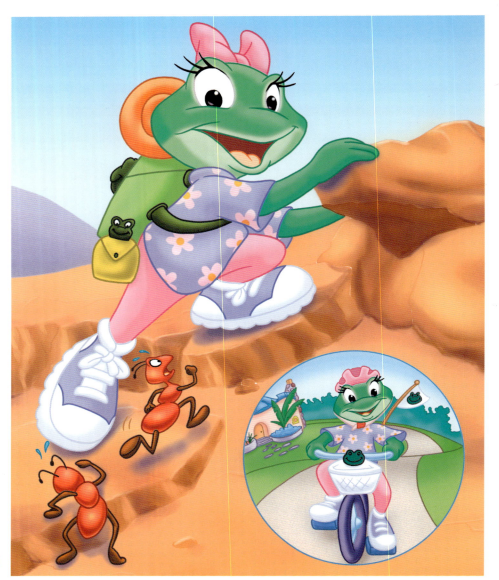

She will go for a hike and ride home on her bike.

She will go to the ice cream store and then do some more!

"Lil, that is a lot! Lil, you can stop!" said Dad.

"When you come back, we'll have a big snack."

With a hug and a kiss, Lil cannot miss.